Crafting CALM

ART AND ACTIVITIES FOR MINDFUL KIDS

BY MEGAN BORGERT-SPANIOL & LAUREN KUKLA

ILLUSTRATED BY ARUNA RANGARAJAN

beaming books

MINNEAPOLIS

Editor: Rebecca Felix
Design: Sarah DeYoung
Production: Emily O'Malley

Photo Credits

Cover: AmeliaFox/iStockphoto (girl); Andrii Cherniakhov/Shutterstock (red leaf); Brett Holmes/Shutterstock (terrarium); Jan Martin Will/Shutterstock (tree); MaraZe/Shutterstock (bread); Mighty Media (glitter jar, colorful shapes)

Interior: Mighty Media, pp. 1, 4, 20, 24, 32, 36, 38–39, 52, 66, 68, 69, 80; paffy/Shutterstock, p. 11 (girl); RUTiAM/Shutterstock, p. 11 (teddy bear); EA Given/Shutterstock, p. 12; New Africa/Shutterstock, p. 13; hanapon1002/Shutterstock, p. 14 (girl); psy dye/Shutterstock, p. 14 (paint swirls); Jaroslav Monchak/Shutterstock, p. 19 (left, right); Gelpi/Shutterstock, pp. 22–23, 39 (boy); Victoria Shapiroi/Shutterstock, p. 26; YAKOBCHUK VIACHESLAVi/Shutterstock, p. 28; JungleOutThere/Shutterstock, p. 33; OnlyZoia/Shutterstock, p. 34; Tartila/Shutterstock, pp. 38–39; Pat Shrader/Shutterstock, p. 41; gnanistock/Shutterstock, p. 43; Anna Nahabed/Shutterstock, p. 45; DSBfoto/Shutterstock, p. 46 (stones); Hajai Photoi/Shutterstock, pp. 46, 47 (pinecone); naKornCreate/Shutterstock, p. 46 (vine); sangsoda7/Shutterstock, pp. 46, 47 (leaf); Litvinenko Bogdan/Shutterstock, p. 47 (moss, mushrooms); Muanpare Wanpen/Shutterstock, p. 47 (leaf); 9dream studio/Shutterstock, p. 47 (plants); mhatzapa/Shutterstock, pp. 50–51 (music notes); Milica Nistoran/Shutterstock, p. 50 (girl); LightField Studios/Shutterstock, pp. 55, 58; Prokhorovich/Shutterstock, p. 57; Krakenimages.com/Shutterstock, p. 59 (top); Prostock-studio/Shutterstock, p. 59 (bottom); Lovely Mandala/Shutterstock, pp. 64 (main, bottom), 65 (main); Sunny Sally/Shutterstock, p. 65 (top); Africa Studio/Shutterstock, p. 71; KK Tan/Shutterstock, p. 75; Kiselev Andrey Valerevich/Shutterstock, p. 77; FatCamera/iStockphoto, pp. 78–79

26 25 24 23 22 21 20   1 2 3 4 5 6 7 8

Hardcover ISBN: 978-1-5064-6526-5
Ebook ISBN: 978-1-5064-6669-9

Library of Congress Cataloging-in-Publication Data
Names: Borgert-Spaniol, Megan, 1989- author. | Kukla, Lauren, author. | Rangarajan, Aruna, illustrator.
Title: Crafting calm : art and activities for mindful kids / by Megan Borgert-Spaniol & Lauren Kukla, illustrations by Aruna Rangarajan.
Description: Minneapolis, MN : Beaming Books, 2020. | Audience: Ages 8-13. | Summary: "In Crafting Calm : Art and Activities for Mindful Kids, kids engage in and practice mindfulness through fun and easy exercises, crafts, and activities, with the goal of learning a deeper sense of calm, peace, joy, and connection to the world around them, all while improving emotional intelligence, boosting self-esteem, and reducing anxiety"-- Provided by publisher.
Identifiers: LCCN 2020006088 (print) | LCCN 2020006089 (ebook) | ISBN 9781506465265 (hardcover) | ISBN 9781506466699 (ebook)
Subjects: LCSH: Peace of mind--Juvenile literature. | Handicraft for children--Psychological aspects--Juvenile literature.
Classification: LCC BF637.P3 B658 2020 (print) | LCC BF637.P3 (ebook) | DDC 158.1--dc23
LC record available at https://lccn.loc.gov/2020006088
LC ebook record available at https://lccn.loc.gov/2020006089

VN0004589; 9781506465265; SEPT2020

Beaming Books
PO Box 1209
Minneapolis, MN 55440-1209
Beamingbooks.com

Deep Breath In . . .

Life is many things. It can be exciting, saddening, uplifting, and frustrating, all in one day. It's no wonder many of us often feel overwhelmed. It's why a lot of people, young and old, are trying to be more mindful. But what exactly does it mean to be mindful?

You can be mindful just by closing your eyes, taking a deep breath in, and listening to the long breath that flows back out. Try it. Did that make you feel calmer? Now imagine that one deep breath as an entire state of mind. In this mental state, your attention rests in the moment. You are calmly aware of your emotions and physical sensations. This is being mindful.

This book is divided into five mindfulness themes. Each theme features activities and exercises to help you deal with life's high and low points (and all the in-between points). You can read it from start to finish or flip to the theme you feel you need most in this moment. Whether you're feeling angry, happy, conflicted, calm, or anxious, you'll find fun, helpful activities and support in these pages.

chapter 1
Catch Your Calm

Every day, we encounter situations that can upset us. These situations might fill us with worry and panic. Or they might lead us to angry shouting and tears.

And that's not all. There are also times when we find ourselves overcome with nervous energy or excitement. On days like this, we may find it difficult to focus on the here and now.

It's healthy to feel all kinds of emotions. It's also good to respectfully share your emotions with others when it feels right. But when your emotions rise to a point where you might lose control of your actions or where your thoughts feel overwhelming, it's a good idea to pause and take a breath.

This chapter includes activities and exercises to help you slow down and regain control of your behavior or thoughts. Settle your thoughts by making a glitter jar, or shake off tension by twisting like a tree. Find peace while blowing paint, or work out anger as you knead dough. Then, the next time you start to feel swept away by your emotions, you'll know just what to do to catch your calm.

Glitter Jar

Having something to focus on can help you relax when your thoughts start to overwhelm you. Make your own relaxation tool by creating a glitter jar.

STUFF YOU'LL NEED

- Clear jar with a tight-fitting lid
- Water
- Glitter glue
- Glitter

PUT IT TOGETHER

1. Choose your materials mindfully. If you can, use a jar that feels nice in your hand. Pick calming colors for the glitter and glitter glue.

2. Pour one part water and one part glitter glue into the jar. Fill the jar about halfway.

3. Add a few pinches of glitter to the jar. Then fill it the rest of the way with water and screw the lid on tightly.

PUT IT TO USE

Pick up the jar and study it. Notice how it feels in your hands—is it cool or warm? Is it smooth or rough? Turn the jar upside down and set it in front of you. Watch the glitter slowly flow from the top and settle in the bottom of the jar. During this time, try to focus only on the glitter and the way it moves.

The Empty Boat

A parable attributed to Chinese Daoist philosopher Chuang-tzu tells of a man fishing in his boat. As he crosses a river, an empty boat collides with his own. If the other boat had held a driver, the man would have been angry. He would have blamed the driver for the collision. But because the boat was empty, the man remains calm.

This parable teaches us the power of perception. When we come by obstacles, we can choose how to perceive them. We can consider them attacks by others. Or we can think of them as experiences we must work *with* instead of *against*. The Empty Boat parable demonstrates that viewing our trials as empty boats instead of personal attacks can bring us peace and happiness.

Twisting Tree

When we're angry or anxious, we carry tense energy and stiffen up like trees. This playful yoga exercise helps you twist the tension out of your body.

o   Start by placing your feet hip-width apart. Plant your feet firmly on the floor.

o   Next, pay attention to your knees. Let them bend slightly.

o   Now, move your focus to your hands. Wiggle your fingers, then let your arms hang loose at your sides.

○ Slowly begin to twist your torso from side to side, letting your arms swing with it. As you do, remember to keep your feet planted, knees slightly bent, and arms loose.

○ Once you feel comfortable with this movement, pick up your pace to find a nice rhythm. Then turn your attention to your breath. Let it fuel your movement.

○ As your body loosens up, let your arms collide with your body as they swing. Feel any tension travel up your spine and out your twisting limbs. If you're feeling really relaxed, close your eyes!

○ After a minute or two, slow your twist until your arms rest at your sides. Bring your feet together and your hands together at your heart. Take a deep breath in through your nose and slowly let it out through your mouth.

How do you feel?

Buddy Breathing

We don't often notice the way we breathe. But doing so can turn our attention inward and calm our minds. This easy exercise lets you focus on your breath with the help of a buddy.

○ First, pick out your buddy. This could be a stuffed animal, a toy figurine, or a small pet that can sit still.

○ Next, lie on your back on a flat surface. It's helpful to do this activity on a firm floor instead of a soft couch or bed, but make sure you feel comfortable wherever you are. If you'd like, place a pillow under your head or knees. You can also bend your knees and plant your feet.

○ Place your buddy on your belly, just above your belly button. Then take a deep, full breath in through your nose. Feel your belly rise and watch your buddy rise with it.

Belly Is Best

Many of us develop a habit of breathing into our chests. This is often the result of feeling stressed. The Buddy Breathing exercise encourages belly breathing. Belly breathing is deeper and fuller than chest breathing. It slows the heartbeat and can lower blood pressure. So when you're feeling stressed, imagine your buddy encouraging you to breathe into your belly!

- To exhale, let your belly fall and let the air in your lungs rush out through your slightly open mouth. Watch your buddy sink with your belly.

- Keep breathing in and out so your buddy moves up and down. Try to continue for three to five minutes.

Soothing Oobleck

Focusing on tactile sensations gives our worried minds a break. Oobleck is a substance that's not quite solid and not quite liquid. Mix up this soothing goop to touch and squeeze.

STUFF YOU'LL NEED

- Cornstarch
- Warm water
- Food coloring
- Measuring cups
- Measuring spoons
- Mixing bowl
- Mixing spoon

PUT IT TOGETHER

1. Pour two cups of cornstarch into the mixing bowl.

2. Measure one cup of water.

3. Choose a color that you find calming. Squeeze a few drops of the food coloring into the water.

4. Pour the colored water into the mixing bowl. Use the spoon to combine the water and cornstarch.

5. Use your hands to test the goop's consistency. Grab a handful and try to squeeze it into a ball. Does the goop feel like a solid? Open your hand. Does the substance ooze into a liquid? If so, you've made oobleck!

6. If the substance doesn't ooze into a liquid, it is too dry. Add one tablespoon of water at a time until you have the right consistency. If the substance is so watery that it doesn't feel like a solid when you squeeze it, add one tablespoon of cornstarch at a time until you have the right consistency.

PUT IT TO USE

Now that you've made oobleck, it's time to play! How does the substance feel when you poke it hard with your finger? How does it feel when you slowly ease your hand into it? Pick up oobleck and watch it move through your fingers. Focus on how the goop looks and feels as you interact with it.

For more mesmerizing oobleck play, try making three separate colors of oobleck. Drop the different colors together on a tray and watch how they meld together!

Peaceful Paint Blowing

Find peace as you watch colors swirl together in a blown-paint masterpiece. To turn this exercise into an art project, pour your paint onto a canvas instead of into a tray.

STUFF YOU'LL NEED

- Washable paint
- Water
- Clear plastic cups, one for each color of paint
- Stir sticks
- Tray or rimmed baking sheet and small canvas
- Straw

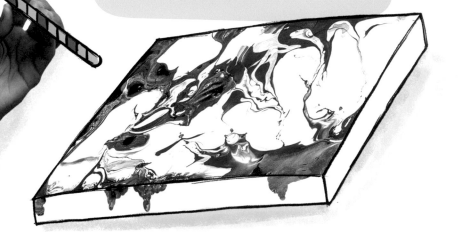

PUT IT TOGETHER

1. Combine equal parts washable paint and water in a plastic cup. Stir to mix.

2. Repeat step one for each color of paint you plan to use. Three is a good number of colors to start with.

3. Carefully pour your colors into the tray. Be mindful about the way you pour each color. Choose any pattern you'd like. Watch the colors swirl together. NOTE: If you are using a canvas, place it on a rimmed baking sheet before you pour the paint.

PUT IT TO USE

Hold the straw a few inches from the surface of the poured paint. Gently blow into the straw. Watch how the paint colors swirl together. How does using your breath this way make you feel?

If you didn't use a canvas but would like to capture your blown-paint masterpiece, gently place a sheet of paper on the surface of the paint. Then carefully lift the paper and flip it over onto newspaper to dry.

Zen Garden

The term *zen* is often used to describe a state of calm in which one's actions are guided by intuition. This activity creates conditions that make such a state possible. Can you find your zen?

STUFF YOU'LL NEED

- Colored sand
- Shallow bowl or container
- Wooden skewer or pencil

PUT IT TOGETHER

1. Fill the bowl with sand.

2. Notice how the sand feels. Run your fingertips over its surface. Scoop up a handful of sand and let it fall through your fingers.

3. When you're ready to make your garden, pick up the bowl and give it a gentle shake to even out the surface of the sand.

PUT IT TO USE

Use the wooden skewer or pencil to make designs in the sand. Start by drawing a pattern in the center. Then draw a new pattern around it. Keep working your way out from the center, drawing whatever shapes and patterns come to you.

Make Your Own Sand!

You can make your own version of colored sand using table salt and food coloring. Just pour the desired amount of table salt into a zippered plastic bag. Add several drops of food coloring. Then press all the air out of the bag and seal it. Knead the bag until all the salt is colored. Open the bag and let the salt dry out before using it.

Zen Buddhism

The Zen garden dates back to the rise of Zen Buddhism, a religion that values meditation. Zen gardens originated in medieval Japan. Hundreds of years ago, Zen Buddhist monks began creating small, simple gardens of sand and stones. The gardens used natural elements to inspire a meditative state.

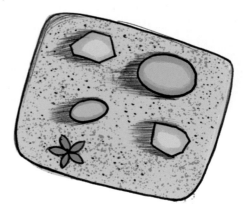

17

Knead to Relax

Are you feeling angry? Work out the negative energy in a productive way. Knead dough to clear your head, and then bake it into tasty bread!

STUFF YOU'LL NEED

- ½ cup sugar
- 2 cups warm water
- 1½ tablespoons active dry yeast
- ½ tablespoon salt
- ¼ cup vegetable oil, plus extra for oiling
- 5 to 6 cups flour, plus extra for surface

- Large mixing bowl
- Whisk
- Wooden spoon
- Towel
- Two 9x5-inch loaf pans
- Oven
- Oven mitts
- Adult helper

PUT IT TOGETHER

1. In the mixing bowl, whisk together the sugar, water, and yeast. Let the mixture stand until bubbles form, about five minutes.

2. Whisk the salt and oil into the yeast mixture.

3. Use the wooden spoon to stir the flour into the yeast mixture, adding one cup at a time.

4. When a soft ball of dough has formed, remove it from the bowl and place on a surface covered in flour.

5. It's time to knead! Start by taking the far edge of the dough and folding it over itself toward you. Then press the heel of your hand into the dough to push it away. Rotate the dough a quarter turn and repeat this process. Knead for eight minutes, sprinkling the surface with more flour if the dough begins to stick to it. Roll the dough back into a ball.

6. Clean out your mixing bowl. Then use a paper towel to coat the inside of the bowl with a thin layer of vegetable oil. Place your dough in the bowl. Rotate the ball until it is covered with oil.

7. Cover the bowl with a damp towel and set aside for about one hour. The dough will rise. It should double in size during this time!

8. Turn the bowl over to place the dough onto a lightly floured surface. Knead the dough briefly to remove air bubbles.

9. Divide the dough in half using your hands. Roll each half into the shape of a loaf. Place each shaped loaf into an oiled pan.

10. Set the pans aside for 30 minutes to let the dough continue rising.

11. Heat the oven to 350°F. Bake the dough until the tops are golden-brown, about 30 to 40 minutes. Wearing oven mitts, tap the tops of the loaves with the wooden spoon. The bread should sound hollow when you tap it. Remove the bread from the pans and place on wire racks to cool.

chapter 2

Examining Emotions

Joy, sadness, anger, fear, disgust—these are just some of the emotions you might experience. Human emotions can vary from day to day, from hour to hour, and even from minute to minute. So many emotions changing so often can be overwhelming.

By learning to recognize your emotions, you'll understand yourself better. You can also better manage how you respond to your emotions.

The exercises and activities in this chapter will teach you to examine your emotions. Before you know it, you'll be an emotion expert!

Let It Rain

Emotions can be tricky to pin down. Recognize them more easily by assigning them physical characteristics, such as colors.

STUFF YOU'LL NEED

- Marker
- 3 small, disposable cups or jars
- Large, clear glass
- Small pebbles
- Water
- Food coloring in four colors
- Shaving cream
- Eye dropper or syringe

PUT IT TOGETHER

1. Think about three emotions you've experienced recently. Draw an emoji representing one of the emotions on each of the three cups.

2. Place pebbles in the bottom of the large, clear glass.

3. Fill each small cup half full and the large glass three-fourths full with water.

4. Think about which color most accurately represents each emotion you drew. Squeeze several drops of that food coloring into that emotion's cup. If you feel the emotion strongly, add extra drops to make the color more vibrant. Repeat with the other colors and emotions.

5. Place a dollop of shaving cream on top of the water in the large glass, making a cloud.

PUT IT TO USE

o Use the eye dropper to drop the colored water onto the shaving-cream cloud.

o Watch the colors sink slowly through the cloud and "rain" down onto the pebbles below. Imagine that each "raindrop" is an emotion drifting from your brain, through your body, and spreading out into the world around you. Watch the drops of color settle into the pebbles. Observe and acknowledge each emotion without judgment.

Mood Art

We can't control our emotions. But we can control our responses to them. For example, instead of hitting your little brother when you are angry at him, you could leave the room to cool down. Sometimes, the first step toward managing your responses to emotions is to allow yourself to fully experience your emotions in a safe and healthy way.

STUFF YOU'LL NEED
- Markers or crayons
- Paper

PUT IT TOGETHER

1. Identify a few colors of markers or crayons that represent the emotions you are experiencing at this moment.

2. Imagine that each color is an extension of yourself. Identify where on your body you are physically experiencing each emotion. Then visualize the color traveling from that place in your body to your shoulder, down your arm, hand, and fingers, and into your marker or crayon.

3. Scribble with each color on the paper. Don't focus on creating a picture or scene. Just color. Envision the color as your emotion spilling out onto the page. As you scribble, allow yourself to fully experience and embrace each emotion without judgment.

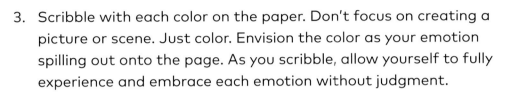

Color Psychology

Many people believe certain colors can trigger specific emotions. Cool colors, such as blue and green, are thought to be calming and relaxing. Warm colors, such as red and orange, are thought to spark energy. Looking for a burst of creativity? Some people recommend gazing at the color purple!

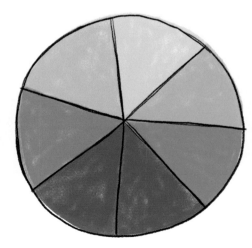

Emotional Case Study

It's impossible to turn off your emotions. But detaching from them can be an excellent first step toward understanding why you might be feeling a certain way. Bring out your inner scientist and examine your emotions.

STUFF YOU'LL NEED

- Object of your choice
- Clear glass jar or bottle
- Pencil and paper

PUT IT TOGETHER

- Select an object to represent an emotion you are experiencing. Place the object in the glass jar.

o   Settle in and observe the object/emotion as if you were a scientist observing an interesting specimen. Write down your observations in a scientific manner, without judgment. You might note how the appearance of the object relates to your emotion, or how the object's purpose or personal meaning to you relates to the emotion. You may even hypothesize what triggered that emotion.

Life without Anger?

In the 1960s, anthropologist Jean Briggs spent seventeen months in Canada's Arctic Circle living with the Inuit people. During this time, Briggs noticed something that seemed strange to her. Her presence certainly disrupted the Inuits' way of life in a manner that would have been frustrating for anyone. But her adopted family never seemed angry with her. In fact, they never seemed to show anger at all!

Briggs soon realized that the Inuit weren't actually living without anger; they were simply managing their response to emotion effectively. When an igloo was accidentally damaged, the Inuit simply said, "Too bad." When a newly made fishing line broke, the Inuit fixed it without complaint. Briggs noticed that Inuit parents never yelled at or scolded their children. Instead, Inuit parents taught their children correct behavior through stories. As the children grew, they learned to express their anger in a calm and productive manner.

Walk the Walk

We often feel our emotions in our bodies. Because of this, we can use our bodies to manage our emotions. Try this exercise to see how the way we move affects the way we feel.

- Walk across the room, using your normal body posture. As you walk, pay attention to how you are feeling at that exact moment.

- Cross the room again, but this time slump your shoulders and keep your face down. How does walking this way make you feel?

- Now walk across the room again, but this time, lead with your chest. Puff up your chest and push your shoulders back. Do you feel any different?

- Repeat this walk again and again, leading with a different part of your body each time. Notice how each change in posture affects the way you feel.

○ Use this trick as a secret weapon to better control your reaction to emotions. For example, if you are feeling anxious, walk with the posture that makes you feel most confident! If you are feeling angry, walk with the posture that makes you feel calm.

Improvisational Theater

Many actors and comedians get their start in improvisational theater, or improv. During an improv show, the actors work together to create characters and storylines on the spot, with no script. Improv actors often use posture and body language to develop new characters and express emotions.

"I do a weird thing when I am nervous where I tilt my head back like I am super confident. This is my attempt to fake it until I make it."

—actress and comedian Amy Poehler, from her book *Yes Please*

Emotional Support Plant

Pets often provide their owners with comfort and companionship. But for some pets, this is an actual job. Emotional support animals are special pets prescribed by therapists and doctors to help their owners through life's challenges. If the work and responsibility of owning a pet isn't right for you, create your own emotional support plant to play a similar role!

You Got This!

Have a GREAT Day!

STUFF YOU'LL NEED

- Hardy, easy-care plant such as a succulent or (not-too-spiky!) cactus
- Wooden craft sticks
- Arts-and-crafts supplies, such as googly eyes, foam, markers, glue, paper, or anything you have
- Wooden skewers

PUT IT TOGETHER

1. Research plants that are easy to care for. Learn how much light, water, and heat these plants need to survive. Then choose a plant that is right for your environment.

2. Think of facial expressions that will lift your mood when you are experiencing certain emotions. Use the arts-and-crafts supplies to decorate a craft stick with each expression. You can even attach word bubbles to wooden skewers with phrases to help boost your mood.

PUT IT TO USE

- Care for your plant according to the instructions you researched.
- Put your plant pal to use anytime you need help handling a certain emotion. When you feel overwhelmed by a specific emotion, choose a craft stick that will lift your mood, and insert it carefully into the soil.

Heart on Your Sleeve

It can be tough to talk about your emotions. Creating bracelets to represent different emotions is a healthy way to recognize—and not bury—the emotions. Wear the bracelets proudly for the world to see, or use them more privately to try to turn a bad day around.

STUFF YOU'LL NEED

o Beads in many colors

o Elastic string

o Scissors

PUT IT TOGETHER

1. Assign an emotion to each color bead. For example, blue could be peaceful, orange could be hopeful, and purple could be empathetic. Use whatever colors make sense to you.

2. Tie a knot a few inches up from one end of the elastic string. Then, string on the beads. Use a single color, or mix and match the colors to create combinations of emotions. When the beaded part of the bracelet is long enough to wrap around your wrist, tie a knot. Trim extra string a few inches from the knot. Then tie the two ends together.

3. Make several bracelets, creating new designs to represent different combinations of emotions.

PUT IT TO USE

You can use your bracelets in different ways:

○ Express yourself! Talk to your family and friends about what the colored beads represent. Encourage them to ask you questions when they see you wearing the bracelets. This can help start a conversation about the emotions you are experiencing at a given time.

○ Wear the bracelets for emotion aspiration! Put on the bracelet that best represents the emotions you wish you were feeling. For example, if you're stressed, put on a bracelet that represents calm or confidence. If you are sad, put on a bracelet that represents joy.

Chapter 3
Being Here and Experiencing Now

We humans spend a lot of time in the past and future. We replay a frustrating conversation we had two days ago, or we dread the chores we'll have to do after school today. We also often worry about things that *could* happen, but probably won't: *What if I have no one to sit with at lunch? What if people laugh at my new hairstyle?*

Thinking about the past and future is an important part of living thoughtfully. But it can also distract us from what's happening right now. That's why we're often told to "stay present" and "live in the moment." This sounds like good advice. But what does it actually mean?

Staying present means giving your full attention to what you're doing right now. This is easier said than done! Our minds tend to wander without us even noticing. But staying present is something we can get better at with practice. The exercises and activities in this chapter can help you develop the skill of being here and experiencing now.

Mindful Steps

Imagine you're out running errands with a parent or making your way through a crowded mall with friends. In situations like these, many of us start to feel anxious, frustrated, or annoyed.

If you find yourself feeling tense while you're out and about, try mindful walking. Walking mindfully means paying attention to your senses as you move through a space. Ready to try it?

- First, slow your pace as much as you can. It's easier to notice different sensations when you aren't rushing. However, stay aware of the people around you too and be safe.

- Next, turn your attention to your feet. Notice how they feel inside your shoes as you take each step. Is the ground or floor hard or soft? Do your shoes make noise against it?

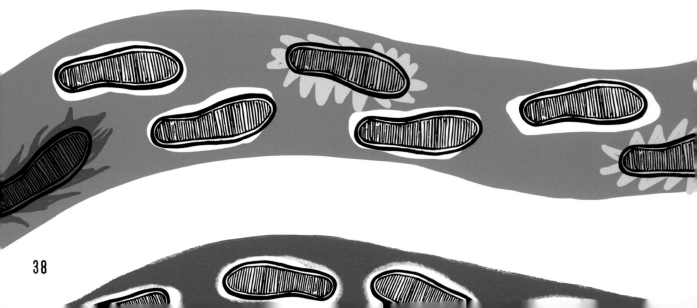

○ Think about your legs. Notice how your knees bend when you walk. Can you feel the skin on the back of your knee stretch as you straighten your leg? Notice your leg muscles tighten and relax as you take each step.

○ Now notice your arms swing back and forth as you walk. What happens when you lift your shoulders up toward your ears and then roll them back? Can you feel your chest and lungs open?

○ Finally, bring attention to your breathing. Breathe in and out with your steps. Try inhaling over five steps and exhaling over eight steps. Adjust this count depending on how quickly you're walking.

○ When your mind starts to wander into a frustrated or anxious place, bring it back to your breath and the sensations of movement.

Five Senses

Have you ever left a situation so you could clear your head? Maybe you went for a walk or listened to music in your room. But sometimes you can't step away from an overwhelming situation.
At times like these, try turning attention to your body. Engage all five senses with this exercise.

- Notice five things you can see.
- Notice four things you can hear.
- Notice three things you can feel.
- Notice two things you can smell.
- Notice one thing you can taste.

Slow Snacking

We often eat with our minds on other things. Maybe we rush through dinner, preoccupied by the pile of homework waiting for us. Or we mindlessly crunch through a bag of chips while watching our favorite TV show. Mindful eating can help you slow down and be more aware of the way you keep your body fueled.

This exercise is meant to help you keep your focus on the food you're putting into your body. A clementine is the example here, but you can use an orange too, or any other snack.

o   Start by holding the unpeeled clementine. Notice its weight. Is the clementine soft or firm? Does it feel smooth or bumpy?

o   Now study the look of your unpeeled clementine. Is its color uniform? Notice little details, like bruises or wrinkles.

o   Start to peel the clementine. As you do so, hold it by your ear. Notice the sounds of peeling the clementine.

- Finish peeling the clementine. Then split off a section. How does it look, feel, and smell? Is it plump with juice?

- Pop the clementine section into your mouth. Before you bite down, let it sit on your tongue. Can you taste anything?

- Finally, bite into the clementine section. Feel it break open. Does the juice make your mouth water? Notice the texture of the clementine as you chew it.

Try to eat the rest of your clementine with the same care and attention you brought to the first bite.

Head-Clearing Kolam

Across the state of Tamil Nadu in southeastern India, many people perform *kolam*, a ritual art of creating patterns out of rice flour. Women make these patterns daily on the ground at the entrances of their homes. The patterns symbolize gratitude and hospitality. Like many rituals, kolam requires care, concentration, and full attention to the present. Try creating your own version of a kolam with flour and a smooth, wet surface.

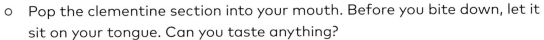

Back to Breath

Do you ever have trouble focusing? Maybe your mind starts to wander while your friend tells you about her weekend. Or maybe you have trouble enjoying a field trip because you're dreading tomorrow's math test.

It's normal for our minds to drift. But sometimes this prevents us from fully experiencing the present. Your mind's ability to focus is like a muscle that needs strengthening. This means you can get better at focusing through practice. And all you need is your breath!

- For this exercise, find a spot where you can sit comfortably. Once you've settled into your spot, close your eyes if you'd like.

- Take a deep breath in and out. This helps you drop into the here and now. Then, go back to breathing normally through your nose.

- Keep your attention on your breath. Listen to the sound of it as you breathe in and out, in and out. What does it sound like?

- Imagine the journey of your breath. Picture the air moving down into your lungs as you breathe in. Imagine that same air rushing out through your nose. Can you feel the air push through your nostrils?

o   Notice how your breath moves your body. Feel your belly stretch outward as you inhale. Can you feel the skin on your back stretch too? What else do you feel?

o   Try to focus on your breath for five minutes. Your mind will probably start to wander, and that's okay. When you notice that it has, gently bring your attention back to your breath. Keep listening to and feeling the sensation of breathing.

Try doing this exercise once a day. In time, you'll notice that your mind can more easily settle into what's happening here and now. As you get comfortable with the exercise, try expanding to focus on your breath for ten minutes.

Nourished by Nature

It isn't always easy to stay mindful and present. There are so many sights, sounds, and devices to pull our minds in every direction! Sometimes it can feel good to leave the modern world behind and be nourished by natural surroundings. Are you ready to escape to nature?

○ Dress comfortably for spending time outdoors. Then head out to a hiking trail, a park, or even your own backyard. Just try to get away from streets and the sounds of cars.

○ Start to move through the natural space. Notice the ground you're walking on. How does it feel? Listen to the sound of each step.

○ Find a spot where you can stop and close your eyes. Take a couple of deep breaths through your nose. Notice the air. Is it warm or cool? What does it smell like?

o   With your eyes still closed, listen to the natural world around you. Do you hear leaves moving in the breeze? Do you hear any birds, squirrels, or other creatures? Is there a sound of rushing water from a nearby stream? See how many different sounds you can identify.

o   Now open your eyes. Look around for a small, loose piece of your surroundings, such as a pinecone, fallen leaf, or pebble. Pick it up and observe it from every angle. Notice how it feels between your fingers. Is it smooth or rough, fragile or strong? Gently place the item back where you found it. Or hold on to it to use in the activity below.

Bottle It Up

You can experience the healing power of nature even when you're indoors. Just bottle it up! Start with a large, clear jar or bottle. Pour a layer of pebbles into the bottom. Then add a layer of charcoal and a thick layer of soil.

Next, you can plant small plants in the soil. You can also add moss, twigs, and any other loose bits of nature you found during your walk. Lightly water the soil, put the top on the jar or bottle, and place your bottled forest near a window.

Constellation Meditation

Did you know that the starlight we see at night has traveled for years—hundreds, thousands, even *millions* of years—to reach our eyes? And because of Earth's yearlong orbit around the sun, the night sky changes slightly with each passing day.

STUFF YOU'LL NEED

- Paper
- Colored pencils

Gazing up at a starry sky can remind us of how spectacular it is in the present. So when weather permits, settle in for a constellation meditation and witness the grand scale of the cosmic here and now.

- Wait for a night when the stars are shining bright and the weather is comfortable. Then grab your supplies and a blanket to keep you warm. Find a comfortable seat outside where you can see the sky.

- First, take in the sky. Notice the brightest stars. Then notice the dimmest specks, the ones you can just barely see. Let your gaze relax and absorb the starlight.

CANIS MAJOR

CASSIOPEIA

- When you're ready, start drawing. Draw whatever you see in the sky.

- As you study the stars, you might come across constellations. The constellations you can see will depend on the time of year and where you live in the world.

- Look at your drawing of the stars. Connect some of the stars to create your own constellation. What will you call your cluster of stars?

URSA MINOR

ORION

CAN'T SEE THE STARS?

It can be difficult to see stars in a big city with many lights. Ask an adult to help you find a local planetarium, observatory, or astronomy club. These organizations can help you see the stars.

Listen Up

Most of the time we're surrounded by noise. Even in a quiet classroom, we might hear a car drive by outside. There are probably sounds from down the hall, like students laughing.

Sometimes all this noise overwhelms us. But we can't always escape to a peaceful place. Instead, we have to cope with the noise. This exercise teaches you to listen in a neutral way. It encourages you to mindfully listen without judging the sounds or letting them affect your mood.

- First, search for a song you've never listened to before, either on the radio or in your own music collection.

- The goal of this exercise is to focus on one aspect of the music at a time. So, start with the vocals, if there are any. Listen for the singers' range, from their lowest notes to their highest notes.

- Next, listen for the instruments playing the melody. Do you hear any string instruments, like violins or cellos? What about brass instruments, like trumpets? Pick out each sound, one at a time, and listen to its contribution to the music.

- Finally, listen for the background beats, like a bass guitar or bass drum.

- As you listen to the music, you might be tempted to decide whether you like it or not. Try to resist this urge! Simply listen to the music without thought or judgment.

LISTENING TO LIFE

You don't have to play music to practice neutral listening. You can do it anytime there's a lot of noise around you! Just listen for each separate component of the surrounding noise. Avoid giving the sounds descriptors such as "annoying" or "distracting." Your only job is to listen!

Chapter 4
Observing Thoughts

You can't control most of what comes your way. But you can control how you react to it. This includes the silent thoughts you have about something. Thoughts may seem harmless, but they have a lot of power. They affect the way we move and carry our bodies. They affect the way we perceive and treat other people. Thoughts can even affect how we feel physically!

It takes practice to become aware of our thoughts. Sometimes this means writing down everything on our minds without editing or judging our words. It also means opening our minds to fresh ideas and insights. Most importantly, it means dealing with thoughts that take over our minds and darken our outlooks.

This chapter is meant to help you step away from your thoughts and observe them from a distance. It offers tools for changing patterns of thinking that do more harm than good. With practice, you'll gain skills to better control what goes on in your mind while still allowing space for it to wander and dream.

Mind Dump

Sometimes we censor our thoughts when they seem too silly or troubling. But acknowledging our thoughts is an important part of knowing ourselves. Here's a chance to dump the contents of your mind out on paper. No judgment allowed!

- Set a timer for ten minutes. Then use this time to freely write, doodle, or sketch anything that comes to mind. Don't worry about how it sounds or looks. Just fill the paper with the contents of your mind, and don't stop until the timer goes off. If your thoughts cover one sheet of paper front and back, keep writing on another!

Bad-Thought Squash

Everyone experiences bad thoughts. These could be negative thoughts about yourself or your abilities. Bad thoughts can also make you think negatively about other people, activities, or experiences.

STUFF YOU'LL NEED

- Ball of clay
- Floor with no carpet

PUT IT TOGETHER

- Mold the ball of clay into a big bug. The more disgusting it looks, the better!

PUT IT TO USE

- Hold the clay bug in your hand and think about the negative thought you've been having. Imagine the thought flying from your head into the bug.

- Keep sending your negative thought into the bug until the bug becomes your negative thought. You are now holding your negative thought in your hand!

- It's time to squash the bad thought. Slam the bug down on the (non-carpeted!) floor to smash it. Or stomp and squish the bug beneath your bare foot. In what other creative ways can you squash the bad-thought bug?

- Once you've squashed your bug, consider your bad thought dead and gone. It can't bother you anymore!

Say It, Think It, Be It

We all know what it's like to have a bad day. It can make us feel grumpy or be in a rough state of mind.

But we can lead our minds in a more positive direction. One way is through affirmations. These are phrases we repeat out loud or in our heads. The words keep us connected to a goal or state of mind we hope to adopt.

You can make an affirmation for any type of situation. Think of the statement that best describes the state you're in. Then think of an affirmation that frames this state in a positive way or ties it to a goal. If you find one you like, write it down and post it where you'll see it every day.

You've studied hard for a test. But on the day of the exam, you wake up feeling convinced you'll fail.

I am smart.
I am prepared.

It's your first day at a new school. You're worried what others will think of you.

I like who I am.
I have the courage to be myself.

You had an argument with a friend. Now you're avoiding this person because you don't feel ready to apologize or forgive.

I am generous.
I replace anger with kindness.

You've experienced a loss. Your best friend moved away. You feel sad and lonely.

I am allowed to be sad.
I will heal in time.

Your math homework always stumps you. You feel like you're falling short despite your efforts.

It is enough to do my best.
With practice, I improve.

Turning BLUE to True

Do you often blame yourself when things go wrong? Do you expect bad things to happen more often than good things? It's not uncommon to have a negative outlook. But this kind of negative thinking takes a toll on both mental and physical well-being. That's why it's important to stay aware of your thoughts. With practice, you can rewire your thought patterns to be realistic instead of negative.

In this exercise, you'll turn BLUE thoughts into true thoughts. The first step is noticing when your thoughts are following one of the patterns below. You can remember these patterns with the acronym BLUE:

Blaming myself—when something has gone wrong, you place full responsibility on yourself and dwell on your mistakes.

Looking for bad news—even though plenty of good things happened, you focus on the one or two bad things and let them bring you down.

Unhappy guessing—among many possible future outcomes, you imagine the worst will happen.

Excessively negative—you perceive minor mistakes or setbacks as total failures.

BLUE thoughts are neither helpful nor realistic. So, turn them into *true* thoughts. To do this, imagine your best friend is the one with the BLUE thought. What would you say to make your friend feel better? Now, say that to yourself!

Blaming myself:
It's all my fault we lost the debate.

It's not all my fault. The whole team is responsible for the loss.

Looking for bad news:
I can't believe I have to clean my room before I can leave the house.

Once I clean my room, I can enjoy the rest of the weekend.

Unhappy guessing:
I'm going to forget my lines.

Even if I mess up, the audience probably won't notice.

Excessively negative:
I'll never be good at math.

I have lots of time to learn and practice more.

61

Ask the Expert

What do you do when something's troubling you? Often, it helps to talk through problems with someone you trust. But sharing what's on your mind can be scary. Maybe you're not sure exactly what to say. Luckily, there's someone you can talk to who will understand your problem more than anyone else. And that person is *you*!

In this exercise, you'll take on two roles.

YOU

You, the person with something troubling on their mind.

YOU+

An older, wiser version of you. Basically, future you. This person is calm, thoughtful, and caring. This person understands your problem but is not affected by it.

SPEAK UP

This exercise is a good starting point to help you sort through your thoughts and feelings. But if something serious is troubling you, like bullying, depression, or anxiety, talk to a trusted adult right away.

Your challenge is to write or act out a scene between YOU and YOU+.
It should look something like this:

YOU state what's on your mind.

I feel like I'm not as cool as the other kids at school.

YOU+ responds with a helpful question about what YOU just said.

What do you feel makes a person cool?

YOU answer the question in as much detail as you can.

Their clothes, their attitude, their hobbies....

YOU+ thinks about what YOU said and responds with a piece of advice or another question.

Tell me about a cool person's attitude. Are they easy to talk to?

YOU →

← YOU+

Continue writing or acting out the scene between YOU and YOU+ for at least two minutes. There is just one rule: Each new response should acknowledge and build upon the previous line. You might find that the older, wiser version of you offers a helpful perspective.

Mind Wide Open

Keeping our thoughts under control is important when they're giving us a hard time. But not all thoughts are bad. Much of the time, our wandering thoughts can lead us to new ideas, perspectives, and goals.
This exercise is meant to keep your visual focus, allowing your mind to relax and wander.

STUFF YOU'LL NEED

- Colored pencils, markers, or crayons
- Printout of mandalas found at https://ms.beamingbooks.com/downloads/BB_CraftingCalm_Mandala-printable.pdf

- Color in the patterns. Focus your eyes on the shapes as they fill with color. Focus your ears on the sounds of the art tools on the paper. And let your mind wander to good places.

Mandala Magic

The patterns in this activity are called mandalas. *Mandala* means "circle" in the ancient Indian language Sanskrit. Mandalas are commonly used as focal points while meditating.

Chapter 5
Capturing Joy and Growing Gratitude

Life is full of surprises. There will be days when you are filled with so much joy you can't stop grinning. Other days you might feel so down you can't muster a smile. There is no way to stop life's ups and downs. But you can learn to appreciate the joy in your life and be grateful for all the good things you have—even when things feel hopeless.

Joy is a state of positive well-being. It is a feeling of contentment with who you are and the life you are living. Unlike happiness, joy is a long-term feeling. It can sustain you even during tough times.

Gratitude is an appreciation for the things in your life. You can be grateful for the experiences you've had that made you who you are. You can also be grateful for the people who love you, the teachers who challenge you, the warm bed that keeps you safe each night, your hope for the future, and much more.

Joy and gratitude are emotions. But you can help cultivate them through choices you make. This chapter will help you practice capturing joy and growing gratitude in your everyday life. You'll learn how to find your inner joy during tough times and appreciate things you may have taken for granted. Joy and gratitude are awesome emotional resources. They can help you navigate life's ups and downs with positivity!

Gratitude Garden

It can be easy to take for granted the good things in life. Take time to appreciate things you are grateful for by making a gratitude garden.

STUFF YOU'LL NEED

- Origami paper
- Large, shallow box, such as a shoebox lid
- Marker
- Craft supplies, such as scissors, paint, tissue paper, tape, and stickers

PUT IT TOGETHER

1. Decorate the box. This will be your garden bed. Be creative!

2. Research different botanical origami projects online or in a book. Look for flowers, cactuses, and succulents. Pick a few you'd like to try. (We've included an example of one origami project on the next page.)

ORIGAMI TULIP AND STEM

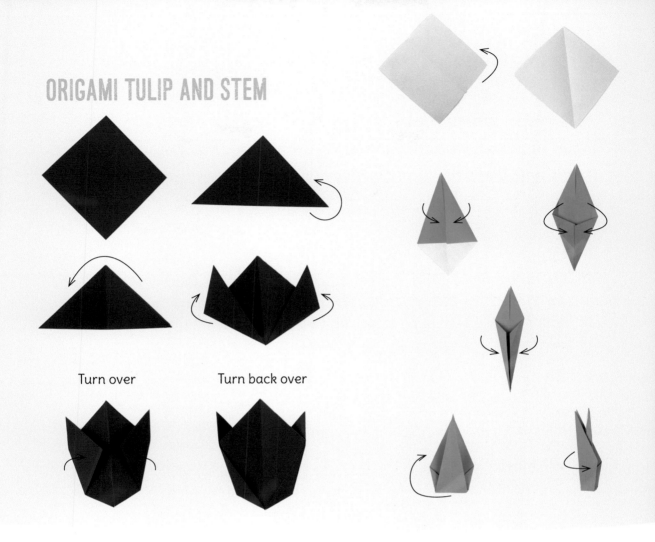

Turn over   Turn back over

3. Before you begin folding, write something you are grateful for on the back of the origami paper. Think about the past, present, and future. What do you appreciate most about your life? What are you most excited for? What makes you feel safest? These can be big things or little things. There are no rules!

4. Follow the instructions you researched earlier and fold your paper plant. When you are finished, place it in your garden bed. Use tape as needed.

5. Make a habit of adding plants to your garden. You could do it every day, every week, or just when you are feeling down. Soon your gratitude garden bed will be in full bloom!

Joy Space

Everyone needs a place they can feel safe and supported. This place should allow you to embrace who you are and be yourself. Create your own space like this to cultivate joy!

PUT IT TOGETHER

1. Identify a space you can make all your own. It could be a closet, a large cardboard box, or even a fort you build. If you are planning to use part of a shared space, such as a living room or backyard, make sure to get permission from anyone else who uses the space too.

2. Turn your space into a cozy retreat. This could include creating cardboard walls or adding blankets and pillows.

3. Consider your senses to fill your space with objects that bring you joy.

   ○ Do you have a favorite scent? Consider bringing in a lotion or scented bar of soap with that aroma.

   ○ Do you like soft light? Consider adding a nightlight to your space.

   ○ Do you have a favorite type of music? Download it on a smartphone or tablet if you have access to one you can use in your space.

   ○ What textures give you joy? Maybe you love the feel of a dog's soft fur. Then consider bringing in blankets or pillows made of faux fur.

4. Add any other objects that bring you joy. This could be anything! The important thing is to choose objects that lift your spirits.

PUT IT TO USE

   ○ Whenever you need a spark of joy, take a break in your special space.

The Nordic Art of Hygge

The Scandinavian countries—Norway, Sweden, Iceland, Finland, and Denmark—experience some of the longest, coldest, darkest winters on Earth. Many people in these countries try to capture joy all winter by embracing the concept of *hygge* (HOO-guh). This is a sense of comfort and coziness that brings a feeling of contentment and joy. People achieve hygge by spending time with their loved ones and enjoying simple comforts, such as wearing a pair of cozy socks or curling up by a fire.

Tree of Belonging

Have you ever felt alone in the world? You're not! According to one 2018 study, nearly half of Americans report sometimes or always feeling lonely. This feeling can be tough to overcome. So, create an artwork to remind you of all the people who love and care about you.

STUFF YOU'LL NEED

- Large poster board or piece of painted cardboard
- Photos
- Art supplies, such as paint, markers, stickers, glue, double-stick tape, scissors, and construction paper

PUT IT TOGETHER

1. Make a list of all the people in your life who love and care about you. Start with your family; then friends; then other adults, like teachers, coaches, neighbors, old babysitters, and anyone you can think of!

2. Organize your list into categories, such as friends, family, neighbors, teachers, and coaches.

3. Draw a big tree trunk on your poster board, or cut one out of construction paper. On the trunk, write your name and paste on a photo of yourself.

4. Add the tree's limbs.

5. Cut leaves out of construction paper. Use one color for each category on your list. On each leaf, write one name from the list. Include a photo if you like.

6. Time to attach the leaves! But before you add each leaf to the tree, hold it for a moment. Close your eyes and picture the person. Think about the ways they have shown you they care. Then paste the leaf to the tree.

PUT IT TO USE

o   Hang up your tree where you will see it every day. As time goes by, you'll likely think of more people to add. Let your tree grow!

"The really wonderful thing that happened to me when I was in space was this feeling of **belonging** to the entire **universe**."

—Astronaut Mae Jemison

Ten Ways to Spread Joy

Doing kind things for others is an easy way to cultivate your own joy. Try out the five random acts of joy-sharing below. Then add five of your own ideas to the list!

HOLD THE DOOR OPEN FOR SOMEONE BEHIND YOU.

GIVE A STRANGER A COMPLIMENT.

MAKE A MUSIC PLAYLIST FOR YOUR PARENTS OR GRANDPARENTS.

SMILE AND WAVE AT SOMEONE WHO ISN'T EXPECTING IT.

SAY SOMETHING KIND TO A FRIEND OR A FAMILY MEMBER.

Ten Ways to Show Gratitude

Expressing gratitude can help bring you joy. Try out the ideas below. Then add five of your own ideas to the list!

1. Thank a friend for something they did that really stuck with you.

2. Tell your teacher how much you appreciate the work they do.

3. Write a thank-you note to someone who helped you out.

4. Offer to clean up after a parent cooks dinner.

5. Before going to bed tonight, write down five things you are thankful for.

The Science of Gratitude

Some scientists research gratitude. One study involved three groups of people. Each week, the people in one group made a list of complaints they had. Another group made a list of events that had occurred, with no positive or negative judgment. A third group wrote down things they were grateful for. After a few months, the people in the third group reported feeling more optimistic than those in the other two groups.

What Do I Like Most about Me?

We humans are often self-critical. It can be hard not to be! You are constantly trying to be a better version of yourself, all while trying to be the best friend, sibling, and son or daughter you can be. It's exhausting!

So, take a breath and take a break. Take time to focus on what you like about yourself, right here and right now.

○ Go to a space where you feel comfortable and relaxed. Choose somewhere without too many distractions.

○ Take three slow, deep breaths. Then think through the questions below:

- What do you like most about your physical self?
  hair, eyes, nose . . .

- What do you like most about yourself as a friend?
  good listener, empathetic, loyal . . .

- What do you like most about your personality?
  funny, kind, open-minded . . .

- What skills and talents are you most proud of?
  athleticism, musical ability, academic ability . . .

- What strengths are you most proud of?
  resilience, bravery, imagination . . .

- What attributes or characteristics make you special?
  freckles, problem-solving skills, great at telling jokes . . .

o Go back through the questions again. This time write down your answers on a separate sheet of paper.

o Go through the questions once more. This time imagine how other people in your life would answer these questions about you. Write down their possible answers too!

Thank You, Body!

Have you ever wished your body looked different than it did? Maybe you wished to be taller or shorter. Or that your hair were curly or straight. Most humans have thoughts like this sometimes. They are especially common when your body is going through changes. But we are often too critical of our bodies. So take a few minutes to thank your body for all the good things it does for you!

- On a sheet of paper, draw a picture or paste a photo of yourself. Leave enough space around the image to write eight to ten short thank-you notes to different parts of your body. For example: *Thank you, lungs, for helping me breathe.* Or: *Thank you, tongue, for helping me taste ice cream.*

- Draw lines connecting these positive statements to the related parts of your body.

- Tape the paper and photo to a mirror or somewhere you will see it every day. Let it remind you how lucky you are to be you!

"When you arise in the morning, give thanks for the morning light, for your life and strength. Give thanks for your food, and the joy of living. If you see no reason for giving thanks, the fault lies with yourself."

—Tecumseh, Native American Shawnee warrior and chief

. . . and Breathe Out

Mindfulness is a journey. And it will take you to surprising places. There will be days you feel at peace with who you are and your place in the world. Other days, you may feel completely overwhelmed. This is part of being human.

Though you have reached the last page, let this book continue to support you. Let the techniques you learned help you during life's highs and lows. Go back and redo the activities that were most meaningful to you. Make little changes so the exercises suit you even better.

This book can serve as a continual tool to help you catch your calm, examine your emotions, be here and experience now, observe your thoughts, and choose joy and gratitude. And don't forget to breathe in . . . and breathe out.